A Warrior of Words

Selected Poems by

STEVE HIGGINS

ISBN: 978-93-90601-00-4

First Edition: 2021

Rs. 200/-

Cyberwit.net

HIG 45 Kaushambi Kunj, Kalindipuram

Allahabad - 211011 (U.P.) India

http://www.cyberwit.net

Tel: +(91) 9415091004 +(91) (532) 2552257

E-mail: info@cyberwit.net

Printed at Repro India Limited.

For my mother Mary Higgins, whose heart shines like a beacon, to me.

Contents

That Seed

Time sleeps in the distant desert,
and sitting softly under the yellow sun,
dried and dehydrated,
there is a seed that waits for the rains.
- I am that seed.
I wait for the rains with open hands
And when they wash over me time wakes refreshed
And I'll drink all I need
-I am that seed.
The seed that longs to know
The secrets of this distant desert
And when my bones lie here
And mingle with the sand
The secrets of the desert -and my own- will be one
-I am that seed
that aches for knowledge
and hungers with desire.
Listen now and understand
And know me now for who I really am
-I am that seed

Some Love

Some love is cold, some love is fire
Some love is nothing but sexual desire

Some love is warm some love is born
Some love's a breeze and some is a storm

Some love glimmers in the dark of the night
Some love shines incredibly bright

Some love is unknown, some is foretold
Some love is silver, some love is gold

Some love is spoken, some love is shouted
Some love just happens and you know nothing about it

Some love is trust, some love is dust
Some love's a card game and suddenly you're bust

Some love is a restaurant and a candle lit dinner
Some love is a loser and some is a winner

Some love is a movie watched in the dark
Some love is fumbling in the back of a car

Some love is a tune that you can hum
Some love is a beat banging on a drum

Some love is walking, some love is running
Some love has passed and some is coming

Some love is gay and some love is straight
Some love matures, some turns to hate

Some love is happiness, some love is strife
but love is the reason for living our life

The Cat Across the Road

Everything seemed in order, I suppose, to die
It was a warm enough day;
Certainly

The sun shone and birds sung
Even though birds would cause a feline heart to race
Normally

I've had my fill of life
Of tit bits and cosy sleeps, sometimes in next doors shed
Informally

And I've had my chases and midnight hunts
And I've always remembered my owners and left them a mouse or two,
Naturally

A last cuddle would have been nice
Still, all in all it's been a good life, and I've loved it
Enormously

I've always liked this tree
I can keep my eye on the birds and the sun comes down
Warmly

So now I'll just close my eyes and die
And go on to the next of my nine lives
Expectantly.

The Long and Dusty Road of Life.

A short road, a long road,
A travelled-only-once-road
It's the long and dusty road of life
It's heartache, happiness, and strife

A happy road, a clean road
Is the road that I desire
A cheerful road, a sweet singing music road,
Free from muddy mire

Let my road be a long road,
A fondly remembered high road
And don't let me detour at a crossroads,
Or linger on a lonely road

One day I'll need a fast road, a rushing road
A quickly time is running out road
And I'll breathe my last in a quiet road, a by road
An end of the line side road

For journeys end is a sad road
A goodbye and thanks for all you've done road
A cul-de-sac, an avenue, a long gone distant road,
And as time passes it soon becomes a travelled-long-ago road

The Thunderbolt

You're not expecting the thunderbolt to hit
Then when it does it hits you like a brick
One minute innocent and unmoved
The next incensed with passion and feeling bemused

Lovely face and beautiful eyes
The curve of your body is no surprise
Your smile affects me so, I'm feeling weak
And like a fool I can hardly speak

On some spiritual wavelength I feel we're actually connected
And that's something so very unexpected
Still, I have to speak, there's a moment here I have to seize;
'Can I have a pint of lager love, please?'

Where the River Flows

Let the river of life take me wherever it will flow
Who knows which way the winds of destiny will blow?
Everything is written and we're just passengers of fate
But then again, perhaps we step towards the future that we ourselves create

Let the tides take me where they will
And wash me up on some distant land
Near or far, for me it doesn't matter
Just send me companions who will hold out their hand

Send me a ship and I'll sail her wherever she cares to go
I've sailed in heavy weather and I've sailed in calmer seas
And all I really need is love and affection
And a breath in my sails from a gentle sea breeze

Life cannot hurt me whatever sadness she may bring
For like winter, every sadness passes and gives way to spring
Fate leads the way to the other side of life
And when death claims us, only then we'll see the light.

So for now we'll carry on with the journey of life
And when a time of sadness comes, write it into words
Cut them out and turn them round
and write a happier verse.

Can You Pass the Bread?

Blood rising
Heart pumping
You were the centre of my passion, once
Though now we meet very politely
And exchange pleasantries
And touch on former days,
Lightly

Your husband seems nice
And I like the wine he's chosen
At a very reasonable price
Though you must forgive me for thinking
How I much prefer the red to the white,
Tonight

Blood rising
Heart pumping
Could you pass the bread?
And how much longer can we be gracious
when I'm hanging by a thread?
I'm filled with desire
And thoughts I cannot mention
So,
Can you pass the bread,
Instead?

Do the Best You Can.

Nothing can be heard but the ticking of the clock
The judge sits in judgement
and I'm standing in the dock.
He asks;' what have you done with your life?
What progress have you made?'
Well, I say, I was born and raised in a council house
I went to school and I went to work
I've breathed the air and felt the rays of the sun
And I've shivered in the cold when the summers done
I've swum in the ocean and flown through the air
And ridden a motorbike as fast as I dare
I've slept in a tent in the middle of the night
and awoke when a nightmare gave me a fright.
I'm never so happy as when I'm reading a book
And I can make my own meals -I'm not a bad cook.
I'm not a Prime Minister and I'll never be King
I just bumble along and do my own thing.
I've had marriage and I've had divorce
And neither are something that I can endorse.
I don't owe any money and I've a number of friends
So, on all of these things will my fate depend?
If it's up to you to sit in judgement, go ahead and be my guest
I'm reasonably confident I can pass your test.
Whatever happens; I'm a child of the universe, at peace with my soul
Will the sentence be life: is there a chance of parole?
My evidence now done I stand up straight in the witness stand
And the judge sets me free with a wave of his hand,
'You're free as a bird; your life is your own

Go in search of Happiness and reap what is sown.
You've progressed from boy to full grown man
And played your part in the celestial plan
Go in peace
And do the best you can.'

The Game of Love.

A hundred nights out, a thousand even or more
And yet we meet unknown and unknowing
A hundred bars, a hundred bar maids
A thousand pints of lager
Chit chat and chat up lines unleashed
Smiles flashed, charm dispensed liberally
And all for us to meet, unknowing
Chance, fate, call it what you will
The hidden hand of the universe
Brought us here to meet
To talk and chat and smile
And dance the ritual of love
So now we've met let's enjoy ourselves
For there'll be tears before we're through.

The Secret Of happiness

I was happy and never knew it,
Sad and knew it so well.
Love slipped by though I hardly noticed,
yet love has marked me well.

Winter passed and summer came
yet I was living in the cold.
My love has turned and passed me by
and outside the world grows old.

Happiness has passed for me
For love has cast its spell
I was happy and never knew it
Sad and knew it so well

Winter in My Soul

It's cold outside
And Winter in my soul
The virgin snowfall numbs my thoughts
And my eyes and ears are frozen whole

Still cold and colder still
Passion frozen as passion will
And still the snowflakes fall
As silently as a snowflake tends to fall

As cold as cold can be
And the heat within means nothing
It's the heat from a thousand words in motion
Frozen thoughts, hot emotions

I can't say the words no more
I can't go on with this charade
I'm hardened now to tell the truth
It's over, I'm afraid

So the arctic chill is passed to you
And the winter snowflakes that you brush away
Are tears of sadness in your eyes
Tears that signal love's demise.

Yourself

Never plan anything
That's my motto
And if you can leave something till tomorrow
Then leave it.
Don't think about loved ones
-Love no one
And consider yourself first and foremost
Above everyone and everything.
Don't get involved
And don't feel bad about leaving something
Unresolved.
Any money you make -spend on yourself
And don't start thinking about other people's feelings
Don't get involved with love and all its dealings
No, don't care,
Don't you dare!
Because then you'd have to plan things
You'd have to think about loved ones
And spend money on someone else
And you know how much you think the world of
Yourself.

The King of The Garden

The King of the garden is dead
And now the vultures come
For once before they would fear to tread
But not now, now the King is dead.

The King was a battered mongrel dog
Who kept his enemies at bay
And no cat would dare to enter his domain
Whatever the time of day

The cats roam fearless now
And in the midday sun can quietly lie
Or dance and play upon the ground
Under which the King's bones do lie.

His memory seems to linger though for when I spied a feline gang
And called out 'CATS' as in days gone by
Tomcat, tortoiseshell and tabby too
Pelted hell for leather and rushed away

Now once again they fear to tread
This garden, this hallowed ground
And that mongrel dog, that former King
Who kept this land free from cats -His memory still resounds.

A Bigger Man Than Me.

I always liked the jacket my Dad wore.
One day I found it
hanging lonely and forlorn
In a wardrobe,
and I thought of him and me
and remembered he was a bigger man than me

I tried the jacket on
and felt him close once again.
I always liked the little pocket for a watch and chain
but to my dismay the jacket didn't fit, not at all:
It was too small
Even though he was a bigger man than me.

He went to work every day on his bike,
a fitter man there never was
and every day of his life he spent outdoors,
lifting concrete blocks,
and hammering tarmac:
He was a bigger man than me

So I never got to wear the jacket
except once when I was a lad
when the jacket was twice the size of me.
So today it's confirmed –I stand bigger than my Dad
though in my heart
he will always be a bigger man than me.

The Camper Van.

Another busy day, another busy week
There must be more to life than working week to week.
I'd like to jack the whole lot in and buy a campervan: I'd drive leisurely down to France and maybe even Spain
Nothing would be too much trouble, nothing would be a pain

Some days I'd have baked beans for tea and sometimes fillet steak
And they'll be days when I'm going far too fast so then I'd put on the brake
I'd park up in some quiet spot and contemplate the sky
Pour a glass of cheap red wine and ask the question why

I wouldn't expect any answers to immediately come to mind
So I'd just tend to settle down, relax and unwind
And I don't suppose it'd really matter if an answer didn't come straight away
I can still imagine it being a lovely sort of day

I'd keep a barbeque handy too and when the coals are hot
I'd cook my sausages and burgers with cheese on top
Occasionally I might wonder about the question that I asked
But when I'm busy with wine and cheese that moment might have passed.

And if I was still there at the end of the week
Well, I'd have plenty of wine, and some cheese and ham
They're the things you can store: things you can keep
Especially when you've jacked it in and bought a camper van.

Slow time, Quick time

Slow time, Quiet time
is the way I've lived my life.
I've moved along at an even pace
Life is not a race.

Quick time, fast time,
My life has picked up speed
Life is a midnight express train
And events are lonely stations
passing quickly by

Slow time, quiet time
Is a pace I need again
Summers that last for ever
And friends that never grow old

Quick time, fast time
I'm at the top of the roller coaster,
dropping quickly down.
The pace can never slow again:
Quick time.
End Time.

Life

What is life all about?
I haven't got a clue
I've no idea
What I'm supposed to do

I feel like a passenger
In a bit of a state
I'm just bumbling along
A prisoner of fate

I sometimes wonder
And I need it explained
How life works
Is it preordained?

I've got no agenda
And no design
I keep on looking
But I can't see any signs

So all I can do
Is proceed ahead
Keep on going
Till I wind up dead

Language.

The only thing in life is language
Not love, not anything else
Not tears
Not laughter
But those things may come after
Its words that matter
Because words come from deep within
Because all our thoughts
All our feelings
Are melted down inside our skin
And from our lips come words
Language,
Not love
Not anything else

A Girl Called Pamela Taylor

Pamela Taylor wears chic clothes
Designer labels, anything goes.
Her coat has buttons made of gold
She likes to be noticed, she's bold.

Pamela Taylor wears black boots,
Her body is a gun that shoots.
She's incredibly sexy and overtly erotic
and her taste is impossibly exotic

Pamela Taylor has blue-eyed eyes
and discreetly she enters other people's lives.
She'll trap you with magnetic sighs
and it's yourself you'll probably despise

Pamela Taylor knows all the best wine
and any man she wins in time.
She's every scene-stealer and wheeler-dealer,
And to the social lepers she's a saintly healer.

Pamela Taylor never pays her fees
She opens locks with other people's keys
One look will slice you through if you tell her lies
Or nothing she can't easily surmise.

Action!

Action!
Now there's a word I've longed to say.
Let me be a film director just for a day
I'd bathe my sets with natural light
And keep my close ups tight.
I'd cast a beautiful girl as my star
and keep her key light bright.
She'd be in all my master shots
And I'd fade the soundtrack in so soft.

Action!

(Dissolve shot of Withington hospital)
It's the day a child is born
Cut to a close up of the baby boy
Swift dissolve to the tracking shots of growing up
-Infants, junior and comprehensive schools
-Time to learn the rules
Cut to the wedding day; close up of the bride.
-Tracking shots, panning wide
Mix in all those smiling faces
Hold it as long as you can
before we gently fade in
Divorce, new job, new friends
Life changes, following new trends.

No need for special effects
But this guy is getting older
(And we need the make-up girl)

Especially for the death scene
(This is going to be awesome on the screen!)
Cue the sad music
Close up of the loved one's tears,

-Cut!

All His Things Are Here

All his things are around here, in the wardrobe and in the drawers
The man himself has gone
But all his things are here

Don't put your things in that drawer, that's drawer's already in use
But it's full of the things of a dead man
And he's no longer here.

It's cold out tonight, so very cold, so why not use this scarf?
It's the scarf of a dead man, a man who's passed away
He's hardly going to need it as he's no longer here.

Don't use that glass, there's a man who used to use it
He drank red wine till he passed away,
now he'll never use it again.

All his things are around here, in the cupboards and on the shelves
In the garage there are jars and jars of screws,
Just waiting to be used.

Perhaps it's time to clear his old things out, they'll never be used again.
Death means going away
And never coming back this way.

A Pub I Used To Know.

The polished wooden bar
Is just how I remember.
The optics, the glasses
Everything is the same
The beer and pint pots
Drinks for the masses
And the barmaids smile is just as nice
As a barmaid that worked here thirty years ago
For thirty years ago I knew them all;
Bar men, barmaids
Pot men, and land lords.
Bar loungers, beer drinkers
And Pool players too.
Lunchtime boozers, and officer workers,
Smokers, Layabouts, and loungers
Misfits, gossips, hangers on
Chit chatters, watchers
Early doors drinkers, bring it on.
Pints of lager
Pints of bitter
Gin and tonics
Whisky and dry
Girls in short skirts eyeing up the lads
Lads and their pints, chatting up the girls
Kissing and cuddling
Loves young dream
Drunken words
Arguments slurred
I've seen it all

From the lady in pink who's giving me the eye
To the girl with the cleavage who shrieks
'What are you looking at –and why?'
'Oh don't mind her –she's just a bit pissed'
Says the barmaid as she polishes the bar
'Why don't you have another jar?'
Thanks for the offer I say to my host
But its thirty years since I was a regular here
And the pub's the same but I feel like a ghost.
There's a chill in here, a bit of a freeze
Maybe its time for' last orders please.'

Cannonball.

I'd like to be a cannonball:
Smash through things and knock down walls
I'd leave a trail of destruction in my wake
Before it's even time to take a tea break.

I'd like to drink fifteen pints of lager
And ride through the shopping centre like a knight on a charger
Smashing things merrily as I go
Making a mess with gusto

I'd like to swear loudly in a quiet bar
And drive like a maniac in a bright red car
I'd go the wrong way down a one-way street
And for a quiet guy like me that'd be something of a treat

I'd like to smash windows and cause havoc
Make a lot of noise and start a panic
Then I'd slip on my shoulders my cloak of invisibility
And disappear from the scene, with due humility

The Christmas Tree

It took a while to grow
The Christmas tree, you know
And for weeks it gave us Christmas cheer
Draped with decorations
Befitting the time of year
But now January has come
and the festive season's done
but we've another use for the tree,
we'll chop it into logs
and burn it on the fire.
It's sad really,
because it took a long while to grow,
The Christmas tree, you know

The Coldest Morning.

In the coldest morning
Of a frozen day
There's a teeny tiny kernel of heat
Deep inside your heart
Keep it safe
You might need it
Some day

In the coldest morning
Of a dead relationship
Reach inside
For that tiny kernel of heat.
You'll need it
For that someone else
You'll meet.

When The Holiday Is Over.

Forget the blue skies and the swimming pool
Your desk is all ready so don't act like a fool.

Forget the pavement cafes and *Mademoiselles*
As your computer fires up with a thousand e-mails
Enough to numb the pain
And the nagging desire for a glass of red wine;
Act cool.

Briefings, meetings and folders to review
Memoranda and consultations to plough through

Forget the *camembert* and French bread
Close the door on the *plat du jour*
It's not even lunch and I can't resist
The thought of a cool *aperitif*;
As if . .

Revised protocols need to be sorted
And I see the new software is unsupported

I'll enjoy my lunch in the works canteen
A ham sandwich and a cup of tea
And the memory of a French *bistro* won't even arise
All bustle and chatter and *joie de vivre*
No, not for me

It Doesn't Matter.

It doesn't matter anyway
That something went unseen today.
Everything fades away.

It doesn't matter anyway
That coastal waters washed away
Our footprints in the sandy bay
That yesterday the sun was warm
And the boy next door played on the lawn

It doesn't matter anyway
That much to my dismay
My bicycle was stolen whilst I was away
And last night our neighbour died in her sleep
She would have been seventy-nine today

It doesn't matter anyway
The day before it rained
And when our newspaper was delivered
Some of the pages were stained
The paperboy's bag was leaking, he explained

It doesn't matter anyway
That evil men take human lives
And that innocent people are the first to die
So perhaps it's time to think about the things that matter
Even the smallest things that pass us by

It matters, it matters in every way
That something went unseen today
Nothing fades away.

My Notebook.

Don't throw away my notebook
Don't throw away my world
I've got notes in there that go way back
To the beginning of time

I've got random bits of notes
And partly finished poems
I've got verses and paragraphs
Problems and stratagems

I've got the phone number of a girl
I met in nineteen seventy-nine
And the winning lottery numbers
For quite a period of time

There are verses that celebrate
And others that speculate
Narrative and chronicle
Couplets and limericks

Things that I've forgotten
And things I won't forget
Things that were important
Memories for a day

So don't throw away my notebook
I'm lost without that world
My whole life with annotations
To the end of my time.

On the Bridge.

It was me that found you on that lonely road that night
I spied you on the cameras around midnight
You looked cold on top of that bridge,
I suppose you thought you'd see things in a different kind of light,
Way up on the bridge
In the middle of the night.
The ambulance was on standby anyway
And I know you had your problems
If only you could have let on, hinted to someone
Maybe you wouldn't have given us such a fright
But I prefer to believe you were coming down
And that you tripped or were nudged by the wind
It's a sad place to die in the middle of a road
No one heard you call or shout
And darkness came when the lights went out.

Senna.

Hard and fast and foot to the floor
Burning rubber
Spinning wheels
Yellow Helmet, blue car

Flat to the corner and turn the wheel
Down the gears
Off the brakes
Clip the apex
Hold the road

Tamburello to Villeneuve
Tosa to Piratella
Acque Minerali
Variante Alta
Rivazza to Traguardo
And all over again.

Race leader: the others follow in your wake
They're close behind but never mind:
Listen for the revs
Fourth gear, fifth gear
Sixth gear; brake!

Safety car, slow it down
You're still the number one
Check the tyres, save the fuel
You can win the race, you fool!

The race is on again
Turn up the power
Yellow helmet, blue car
Two hundred miles per hour

Approaching Tamburello
Accelerating through
Turn the wheel; hold the line, even though the car is slipping
You're the best; you know that's true
You can stop the car from skidding

Yellow helmet, blue car
Death on the concrete wall
Red blood, yellow helmet
Dust for a funeral pall

The Champion's day is over
His time has come to an end.
No one remembers the competition
Just his death on television

Signal.

I'm sending out a signal, sending out a call
It's for someone I knew years ago
That's if she's listening at all.

Silent years, lonely years are in between us now
So let us talk, let us bridge the gap
So softly, ask me how

Send me a message, send me a signal, I'll be waiting around
But I'm counting the hours
Just listening for a sound

So listen to my signal, listen to my call
I long to hear your voice
Hope you're listening, after all.

The Child Inside.

The child inside of me
Is the child I used to be.
The hopes and fears
Of the child inside
Are still alive in me,
And every day, in every way
I'm still the child inside.

The child inside shapes the view
Of the world I see today
And the eyes of the child
Are round and wide
And I will be their guide.

For the child inside everything is new
Every road and every lane
We've yet to travel through
The tiny hands of the child inside
nestle inside mine
And every soul that I might touch
Will touch the child inside.

The child inside is innocent
And free of any stain
But we are linked by deeper bonds
our soul is the very same.
The child inside
Is me inside,
the conscience within my pride.

Thoughts Are Things.

Thoughts are things
Not things that disappear when your mind is closed
Or a wave of energy that fades away
Oh no, thoughts are things
They're here to stay

So when I see you face to face
I take that vision place to place
And when I'm tired and sleeping fast
That thought is with me in my dreams
Because thoughts are things
They're here to stay

So that thought, to me, is like a precious stone
I'll wear it on a ring around my finger
And with every glance I take the more its lustre lingers
I don't expect it to ever fade away
Oh no, thoughts are things,
They're here to stay.

Universe.

The wailing wind is in my breath
And in my dreams I see the silver moon
My smile is the face of the summer sun
And daybreak stirs my waking soul
When sadness comes my tears are one with the pouring rain
And the blood within my veins runs deep within these hills
This Earth is at the centre of the gift of life
And when I die she folds my bones within her arms
While my free spirit soars above
High above the wailing wind in death

The Top of the Hill.

I'm going to the top of the hill
And by hook or by crook
I'll get there,
I will

It's sunny at the top of the hill
With sun beds and free beer
And friendly people
With goodwill
And cheer

When I get there
I'll relax for a while
And contemplate my climb.
For when I've reached the summit
Things will never be the same
And I can only go downhill
Again.

So I'll lord it for a while,
Let them treat me like a king
For one fine day they'll unmask me
And call me 'imposter!'
But I'll have had my day at the top of the hill
Somehow I'll get there,
I will.

The Rain

The stream becomes the river
The river becomes the sea
And the rain that washes over me
Washes into the sea.

For you are my rain,
My river and my stream
And I am the fisherman
Who loves you in his dreams.

So when I wake I'll hold you
And take away your pain
Love can wash the pain away
Like dust in the pouring rain.

The stream becomes the river
The river becomes the sea
And all our sins are washed away
When the rain washes over me.

The Background Guy

That ongoing story that I call my life
Is nothing but a total tangled mess.
It's a disaster area; a no-go zone,
And sometimes I feel like staying at home.

It's a rambling narrative with a spot of romance,
Love and sadness and elements of chance.
The day will come when all will be resolved,
And the pain and sadness will just dissolve.

If you see the film version, don't bother to watch
If you see it in a bookshop, it's one to dodge.
It's an ordinary story of an ordinary guy,
Who can't find answers to the question; why?

In the theatrical production that I call my life
I've played lead roles and bit parts too.
I'm not the hero and I'm not the villain,
I'm a sort of background guy, just filling in.

But the day will come when everything stops.
When the script runs out and the curtain drops
So we'll clean off the make-up and learn new lines
Look out for another production, sometime.

Poem for Brussels.

Blow me up
Blast me against the wall
Burst me with bombs and guns into a thousand pieces.
Shoot me down dead
With bullets to the head
And while my blood runs into the sand
Just think for a moment
That you could have shook my hand,
Said hello,
Fired words at me
Instead of bombs.
You could have screamed at me if you wanted,
Shouted, screeched and yelled.
You could have blasted me with a thousand insults
argued, blarneyed and cajoled,
Brought debate and contention to a head.
Instead,
We all know now that blood runs red
When innocent people lie dead.

That's Enough

I don't need applause
Or any kind of praise
I don't need affirmations of love
Just a sign, that's enough.

I don't need platitudes
Or fake understanding.
I don't need speeches
Just a word, that's enough.

I don't need your tears
I've got tears of my own
And I don't need your anger,
Just advice, that's enough.

I don't need your sorrows,
I've sorrows of my own
I've got sadness and heartache
Up to here, that's enough

I don't need your gratitude
Or any sort of thanks.
I just need you and your love,
Just you, that's enough,

Tap, Tap, Tapping My Way.

I'm caught up in the fog
I've got my hands out
Feeling my way like a blind man in a haze
Tap, tap, tapping my way along,
Through life.

I don't really know what I'm looking for
But I keep searching
I'm like a blind man fumbling in the dark
And I sometimes think I need an instruction book
So I can be flick, flick, flicking,
Through life.

There are times; I guess it's my lot,
When I don't understand the plot.
I'm going backwards and forwards
Trying to understand.
Fast, fast, forwarding
Through life.

One day there'll be a break in the fog
And I'll see the sun,
But when the answers won't come
I'll dream harder,
Borne back to the past by memories
Back, back, back,
Through life.

I Hope the Train Breaks Down.

I hope the train breaks down
Before the end of the line.
Then again; that's a bit of a foolish thought
For sooner or later
We'll get to the end,
In time.

I'm not in any hurry
To get to journey's end
I might even change trains at the next station
I'm not quite ready
For the end of the line.
This time.

So I'll carry on with my trip
And I'm enjoying my travels
Plenty of stations to call at
While life unravels.
I'll get to the end of the line,
Sometime

The Sands.

I made sandcastles here as a lad.
I've walked and ran with the dogs,
Faced the rain and the blustering winds,
Dozed in the summer sun,
And beachcombed.

When I die, burn my body like a Viking God
And bring my ashes to the sands.
When the tide turns and the wind blows hard
Then empty my remains.
Let the wind take them across the waves;
And watch while the sea foams.

Once more I'll smell the sea smell
And hear the sea birds squawk.
Though when the wind whips up the sand
It'll sting my legs no more
But I'll wave a ghostly hand at all that I was,
And forever roam this shore.

The Same Day.

Some days I look at the mantelpiece
Where the dust gets thicker and the cobwebs grow
I'm not sure what to do about it, you know.

Every day seems like the same day
And even though it's sunny outside
Sometimes the clouds get in the way

I watch the TV but I don't always take it in
And the flickering colours and sounds
Are something I don't want around.

Every day seems like the same day
The sounds and colours all merge
I feel like I'm living underwater and life has all submerged

Have I eaten my breakfast?
Have I taken my pills?
Where's my cardigan? I'm feeling the chills.

Every day seems like the same day
Sometimes it's warm and sometimes it's cold
Nothing changes while I sit here growing old.

President Kennedy

President Kennedy, won't you come back to me
Tell me all you know,
Tell me about Marilyn Monroe

Tell me about Oswald, Ruby and J Edgar Hoover,
The CIA and their secret manoeuvres
Tell me about the Oil men and the FBI,
The five-star generals and the new frontier.

Tell me about the missile crisis and the U2 flights
Tell me about Cuba and the Bay of pigs
Tell me about Civil Rights and Martin Luther King,
Bobby and Lyndon and that sort of thing

Tell me about Castro and Khrushchev and the missile crisis
The Green Berets and Vietnam
Tell me about Jimmy Hoffa and his crooked schemes
I'm sure you know just what I mean.

President Kennedy, won't you come back to me
Tell me all you know,
But most of all
Won't you tell me about Marilyn Monroe?

Mother

She's a fading flower
Not nearly as bright as she used to be
Though now she shines in a different way
Though she always shines to me

She's filled with determination,
And don't try to tell her what to do:
She's stubborn,
And she'll do what she needs to do

The day I can't do my shopping
Is the day I'm finished, she says.
And she eyes me with disdain
Because it's her job to make the tea,
Not mine.

She's a fading flower
Not nearly as bright as she used to be.
Though her heart shines in the darkest night
Like a beacon, to me.

A Thousand Years or So

It's happened all before:
People lived and loved
A thousand years ago,
Or so.

They had petty squabbles
And were late for work
They spent money they didn't have
And bought things they didn't need

They lived and died
And laughed and cried
A thousand years ago,
Or so.

Men chased their lovers
And they wined and dined
And made love under the covers
Kings and queens and Emperors
Ruled over others

Laws were made
And laws were broken
And promises were made
And writers wrote of many things
And plenty of words were spoken.

It's happened all before
And the world was made anew
It's been remade a thousand times
A thousand times, or so

The Thoughts Inside my Head.

Do not presume to know
The secrets of my heart
Neither could you hope to understand
The thoughts inside my head

Don't expect a welcome
As you try to probe inside
For the thoughts that are mine only
Are the thoughts inside my head.

So don't be so upset
When your questions are unanswered.
My heart is locked and forged with steel
As are the thoughts inside my head.

And don't presume to know me
Or the workings of my heart
It's a safe space, a no-go zone,
Until I decide to let you know

The thoughts inside my head.

I'm a Warrior of Words

I'm a warrior of words
And I'll fight you to the death
With my pen
For the right to speak my thoughts aloud.
I'll tread the boards and stand before the crowd
Though I might need a moment to gather my thoughts
And choose a subject for an almighty discourse;
Life, Liberty and freedom, the usual sort of thing
I'll have to wing it: speak off the cuff
I may even throw something in about love.
Either way, I'll use lots of words,
Big ones, small ones: Words I've read in books.
I'll articulate and emphasise
And define and describe.
I'll say something profound
And add a touch of the lyrical;
Something suitable
For a warrior of words.

The Sixtieth Floor

So,
I'm in the elevator
Going higher and higher.
I'm taking the lift to the sixtieth floor
Though I can't really see myself opening the door.

Still,
I often think about reaching that floor
I won't be the first;
People have been there before.
I guess it's all normal for a man of my age
It's like reading a book and turning the page.

So,
I'm taking the lift to the sixtieth floor
I'm making steady pace
One floor at a time.
Be kind of nice to stop off, on the way
They say the thirty second floor is the place to stay

Still,
Life isn't over,
It's a series of steps
And there's bound to be more.
I'm sure there's life after the sixtieth floor.

The Wings of Life

The wings of life grow old
And I cannot fly like I used to do
When I was young and bold

Time is now like a distant summer's glow
And I long for those summers
That once I used to know

Of course, there are still those sunny days
When I pull on my wings and fly,
When I rise up towards the sun and feel her rays

But one fine day I'll rise up and fly so very high
And drop down so very fast
And life will end with a clarion call, not a sigh

The Cycle of Life

It's not death that comes
its life that passes.
And all that's left
must turn to ashes.

The sun will rise
and the moon will pass,
and the next day comes
when the night slips past.

So death cannot come
and make a claim,
for time moves on
and soothes the pain.

The Only Man in the Space Station.

The auto-alarm sounds like a churchyard chime.
And a second seems to take all of time
In the darkness within the middle of a dream
I can see faint traces on the scanner screen

I'm the only man left in the space station,
and the lights are low as I'm waking
I'll sit back and while away the hours
And check the sky for meteor showers

I'm a lonely man with an amazing view
Though everything I see is in shades of blue.
Later on, I'll take my oxygen pill
When the sky is quiet, and all is still.

The auto-climate is set for a summer Earth day
but the technology guys could never find the way
How to capture the scent of rain?
Or an autumn day in southern Spain?

The memories of Earth still survive
On the day I get back I'll go for a drive
Maybe go for lunch in a country club
Or spend a few hours drinking beer in a pub

You can blow your mind in time,
On the edge of space all the world is mine.
I'm the master of the world, up here in space
I could drop a bomb in the perfect place

But I've no desire to harm the Earth
I'm like a New York cop, I protect and serve
Bombs are bad for the atmosphere
And my job here is to keep things clear

The auto navigator is set in place
And I'm ready for dinner in outer space
I've finished for the day, so I'll just fill in my log
And just imagine a walk with the dog.

Find out more about Steve Higgins by visiting
www.stevehigginslive.com

www.ingramcontent.com/pod-product-compliance
Lightning Source LLC
Chambersburg PA
CBHW050025170726
48282CB00025B/549
9789390601004